Design by TEAMS:
Digital Picture Data Base
Copyright: Andi Bowe 2010
ISBN: 978-0-557-55616-8

WEBQUESTS:

ANDI BOWE
PRESIDENT/FOUNDER

AAA DESIGN SERVICES GROUP
"THE SANCTUARY PROJECT"
College of Synthesis
"NO DESIGN TOO SMALL"

MESSAGEPHONE: 951-452-4794 X1529

EMAIL: SPIRITUALUN2002@YAHOO.

WEBQUESTS:
http://www.angelfire.com/hi3/spiritualun

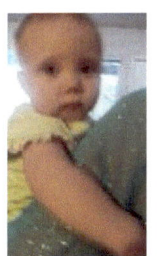

clara bowe in Seattle in 1935

Design by TEAMS:
Digital Picture Data Base
Copyright: Andi Bowe 2010
ISBN: 978-0-557-55616-8

www.ingramcontent.com/pod-product-compliance
Lightning Source LLC
Chambersburg PA
CBHW041114180526
45172CB00001B/237